The Reality of Life after Death

by
Dr. Rodney
Howard-Browne

THE REALITY OF LIFE AFTER DEATH
by Dr. Rodney Howard-Browne

Unless otherwise noted, all Scripture quotations are taken
from the New King James Version of the Bible. Copyright
© 1979, 1980, 1982 by Thomas Nelson, Inc., publishers.
Used by permission.

Scripture quotations marked AMP are from the Amplified
Bible. Old Testament copyright © 1965, 1987 by the
Zondervan Corporation. The Amplified New Testament
copyright © 1954, 1958, 1987 by the Lockman
Foundation. Used by permission.

Scripture quotations marked KJV are from the
King James Version of the Bible.

Scripture quotations marked NIV are from the Holy Bible,
New International Version. Copyright © 1973, 1978, 1984,
International Bible Society. Used by permission.

Contents

CHAPTER ONE

IS THERE LIFE
AFTER DEATH?

There was a certain rich man, which was clothed in purple and fine linen, and fared sumptuously every day: and there was a certain beggar named Lazarus, which was laid at his gate, full of sores, and desiring to be fed with the crumbs which fell from the rich man's table: moreover the dogs came and licked his sores. And it came to pass, that the beggar died, and was carried by the angels into Abraham's bosom:

1

the rich man also died, and was buried;

And in hell he lift up his eyes, being in torments, and seeth Abraham afar off, and Lazarus in his bosom. And he cried and said, Father Abraham, have mercy on me, and send Lazarus, that he may dip the tip of his finger in water, and cool my tongue; for I am tormented in this flame. But Abraham said, Son, remember that thou in thy lifetime receivedst thy good things, and likewise Lazarus evil things: but now he is comforted, and thou art tormented.

And beside all this, between us and you there is a great gulf fixed: so that they which would pass from hence to you cannot; neither can they pass to us, that would come from thence. Then he said, I pray thee therefore, father, that thou wouldest send him to my father's house: for I have five brethren; that he may testify unto them, lest they also come into this place of torment.

Abraham saith unto him, They have Moses and the prophets; let them hear them. And he said, Nay, father Abraham: but if one went unto them from the dead, they will repent. And he said unto him, If they hear not Moses and the prophets, neither will they be persuaded, though one rose from the dead.

—Luke 16:19–31, kjv

When Jesus related this story, He was not making it up to illustrate a point. He was speaking about real people, who actually existed—a *certain* rich man and a *certain* beggar named Lazarus.

Jesus shows us that even though they had both died, they did not simply cease to exist—they could still see, hear, feel, talk, reason, and understand.

Life after death is a reality! It was a reality to Lazarus and the rich man, and it is a reality to every person who crosses over to the other side! There is a real heaven and a real hell, and these are the only two places people will go when they breathe their last breath. There is no other place where one will spend eternity—*and that is a fact.*

Heaven is not a place in your imagination, in your dreams, or in your fantasy—and it's not simply what *you* make it, as some say. Heaven was never in the mind of man, but it has always been in the heart of God. Hell is also a real place. It was not designed for man but for the devil and his angels. Unfortunately, however, people who die without God do end up there.

> THERE IS A REAL
> HEAVEN AND A
> REAL HELL.

You are an eternal being. You and I, right now, are living in eternity. We only have one life to live, and whatever we choose to do in this earthly life will affect our eternal destiny. We only have one life to live, one opportunity to choose our destiny, and whatever we decide and do now is going to count for eternity. The Bible tells us to work out our salvation with fear and trembling. In other words, *this is not a game!* It is very, very serious.

Hebrews 9:27 says, "And as it is appointed unto men once to die, but after this the judgment" (KJV).

There is no chance that you can get your life right with God after you die. Many people play around with the things of God and their salvation, saying, "Oh, it'll be fine. I'll get it right one day. Even when I die, God will have mercy on me." That's a lie from the pit of hell; God's mercy is endless *before* you die, but it's too late afterwards. God gives everyone opportunities to make decisions this side of the grave, not later. It's your choice!

When I was about thirteen years of age, I had an unusual dream. I saw the light of the glory of heaven and the cross at the top of a road. Jesus stood at the side watching as a small number of people made their way up that road. However, the masses were going over a precipice into the horrible chasm of eternal damnation, into the flames of hell. These poor people were laden down with every form of bondage and sin, and because they didn't realize their fate, they were happily headed for disaster. They didn't know they were going into a lost eternity until they stepped over into oblivion.

I was so moved and shaken by this sight that I sobbed and cried out to Jesus, "What are we going to do about these people?"

"I've already done everything I can do for them," He replied.

"Then who's going to tell them?" I asked.

The Lord looked at me and said, "You must tell them! You must tell them! You must tell them!" I wept and sobbed as I told Jesus, "I will tell them! I will tell them! I will tell them!" I awoke to find my pillow soaking wet with my tears.

That was the first time God had ever dealt with me in that way. Before we went into New York City in the summer of 1999, I had a dream that was similar to that one many years earlier. I knew without a doubt that my experience then and the dream I had later were linked together.

God is calling people. He is going to bring them in from a lost and dying world. He is going to bring them out of the kingdom of darkness into the kingdom of light. The harvest is ripe and ready!

> And He said, "The kingdom of God is as if a man should scatter seed on the ground, and should sleep by night and rise by day, and the seed should sprout and grow, he himself does not know how. For the earth yields crops by itself: first the blade, then the head, after that the full grain in the head. But when the grain ripens, immediately he puts in the sickle, because the harvest has come."
>
> —Mark 4:26–29

I believe that in these last days it is no longer just the sickle being put in to reap the harvest, but it is the combine harvester! A combine is a huge harvesting machine that threshes and cleans grain as it moves across a field as the farmer reaps his crop. I believe that God's combine harvester is in motion!

Faithful Christians have been crying out to God for souls, and He is answering. We are on the brink of the great harvest of souls that we have all been praying for. Whole cities and towns will be shaken as souls are harvested to populate heaven!

> And as Moses lifted up the serpent in the wilderness, even so must the Son of Man be lifted up, that whoever believes in Him should not perish but have eternal life. For God so loved the world that He gave His only begotten Son, that whoever believes in Him should not

perish but have everlasting life. For God did not send His Son into the world to condemn the world, but that the world through Him might be saved. "He who believes in Him is not condemned; but he who does not believe is condemned already, because he has not believed in the name of the only begotten Son of God.

—John 3:14–18

YOUR DECISION TO FOLLOW CHRIST MUST BE MADE IN THIS LIFE.

Be aware of this eternal fact: if you die without accepting Jesus Christ, you are lost for all eternity without chance of redemption. Your decision to follow Him must be made in this life, on this side of the grave. There will be no opportunity to come back and correct your error. There will be no "Oops, I made a mistake."

The devil has propagated deadly lies that are sending millions of people to hell. Let me warn you of some of them:

1. *Reincarnation (coming back to live life again over and over):* There is no such thing! You will *not* come back to live your life over a second time as another individual or in another form. You only live one life.

2. *Purgatory (a place you go to after you die to wait until you become fit for heaven):* This is not biblical, and no such place exists. There is no place where you can pay penance for deeds done while you were on the earth,

or where after a time of suffering God feels sorry for you and takes you on to your reward.

3. *Annihilation (to cause to vanish or cease to exist):* This means that after you die, your existence—in any form or on any plane—totally ends, and you become completely oblivious with no more consciousness of the physical or the spiritual realm. In fact, people who believe this usually do not believe that the spiritual realm even exists, but they are wrong.

4. *Ultimate reconciliation:* This is the belief that after a period of time, God will suddenly decide that He loves everybody, even the devil, and He will release everyone from hell and send them to

13

heaven! Nothing could be further from the truth.

Tragically, there are people that actually believe these things and stake their eternity on them!

CHAPTER TWO

HELL

Forget what you have seen in the movies. Hell is not a figment of some demented scriptwriter's imagination. It was not invented by Hollywood. Hell is a real place, a literal place. Hell was never intended to receive the souls of men—it was made for the devil and his angels. However, unless man accepts God's plan of salvation and the One that He sent—Jesus—tragically, that is his final destination! We can learn about hell and the fall of Lucifer (Satan) from the prophet Isaiah.

Hell from beneath is moved for thee to meet thee at thy coming: it stirreth up the dead for thee, even all the chief ones of the earth; it hath raised up from their thrones all the kings of the nations. All they shall speak and say unto thee, Art thou also become weak as we? art thou become like unto us? Thy pomp is brought down to the grave, and the noise of thy viols: the worm is spread under thee, and the worms cover thee. How art thou fallen from heaven, O Lucifer, son of the morning! how art thou cut to the ground, which didst weaken the nations!

For thou hast said in thine heart, I will ascend into heaven [so we know hell is beneath us and heaven is above us], I will exalt my throne above the stars of God: I will sit also upon the mount of the congregation, in the sides of the north: I will ascend above the heights of the clouds. I will be like the most High. Yet thou shalt be brought down to hell, to the sides of the pit. [God was speaking to the devil here.] They that see thee shall narrowly look upon thee, and consider thee, saying, Is this the man that made the earth to tremble, that did shake kingdoms; that made the world as a wilderness, and destroyed the cities thereof; that opened not the house of his prisoners?

—Isaiah 14:9–17, KJV

These descriptions of hell bear witness with what people have experienced in modern times. There are accounts of people who have died, and yet God, in His mercy, allowed them to come back. They have said that the instant they left their body, they began to descend...down, down, down.

One preacher describes the near-death experience that brought him to the realization that he needed to accept Jesus as his personal Lord and Savior this way: "I left my body and went down so far that the lights of the earth grew dim above me, and darkness totally covered me all around." He stood at the gates of hell and saw a sight so horrific that he couldn't even fully describe it. He saw giant flames of hell leaping up and heard the agonized screams of the multitudes echoing through the caverns of the damned.

Some people think hell is going to be like a party. "I'll just order a beer when I get there," they say flippantly. Let me tell you boldly and truthfully that there is no beer in hell and there are no breweries. You will not see any houses or streets or mansions, either. Furthermore, there are no cars to drive or water fountains to quench your terrible thirst.

How many movies have you seen where the men are about to blow each other away, and they say so casually to each other, "See you in hell"? Hell is not a place you want to go. It is not even a place where you want to be seen.

Take note of the warning while you can: hell is a place of

torment! It is like a giant inciner-
ator where the flames don't
stop—you just continue to burn
for eternity. (See Matthew 5:22,
Mark 9:43-48.) The Bible also
says that worms will feed on your
body the whole time you're in
hell. (See Isaiah 14:11.)

The world's concept of hell is
incredibly far-fetched! If you have
ever watched a horror movie, put
out by Hollywood, you know they
are conditioning people to think
that hell is just a fantasy place.
Whether they mean to or not,
they're leading people to believe
various myths: that there is no
hell and no life after death; that if
there is a hell, only truly bad
people go to hell; that if you're a
"decent" person, you won't go
there; that you can come back

from the dead if you want to; that you can bargain with God once you reach the other side; that you either have no choice of where you will spend eternity or you alone can make the choice, without the intercession of a mediator or a Savior.

Hell is a place of torment.

People think that hell is a fantasy that will fade away with the movie credits. But do you know what? If they die without Jesus, rather than fading away, hell will be an eternal nightmare that they never come out of. There will never be any change—they are damned forever!

Hell is so serious that Jesus, while He walked on earth, spoke a great deal on this topic to make sure that people were properly warned. Apparently, a certain American state has an, as yet, un-enforced law that says it is illegal to preach about hell because they feel that preaching on hell might cause "duress" and upset people! Did you know that? Even though they have not enforced it, the law gives the authorities the right to walk into any church, where the pastor is preaching about hell, and arrest him!

And horror movies don't cause duress? *Please!* No matter what sewage Hollywood cranks out week after week on television, on cable and in the theaters, they say, "Oh, that doesn't cause anybody stress. It's just entertainment!" Theirs may be fantasy, but they don't want us telling the truth about the real hell. They don't want us to tell the truth of what is actually going to happen. They can throw me in jail, but I'll not stop preaching the truth because God doesn't want people to go to a devil's hell. That is why Jesus came two thousand years ago—so you could have life, and you could have it more abundantly. Hallelujah!

GOD DOESN'T WANT
PEOPLE TO GO
TO A DEVIL'S HELL.

Let's look at the passage in Luke 16 again so that you can get it in your heart: "And in hell he [the rich man] lift up his eyes, being in torments, and seeth Abraham afar off, and Lazarus in

23

his bosom. And he cried and said, Father Abraham, have mercy on me, and send Lazarus, that he may dip the tip of his finger in water, and cool my tongue; for I am tormented in this flame" (KJV). But Abraham told him he couldn't do that because there was a great gulf between them. "And beside all this, between us and you there is a great gulf fixed: so that they which would pass from hence to you cannot; neither can they pass to us, that would come from thence."

What Abraham was saying is that, "Nobody can come to you, and you can't come to us."

The rich man was not about to give up. "All right, then, if you can't do that, I've got five brothers that are alive on the earth. Send somebody back to warn them, 'Don't come here! Don't come here! This is not a place where you want to come.'"

People don't always like to hear about hell. They will not accept the truth about hell, no matter who tries to convince them. In the above Bible passage, Abraham said to the rich man, "If your brothers won't listen to the warnings of Moses and the prophets, neither will they be convinced by someone who was raised from the dead. Even if they begged them, they still would not listen."

And I saw a great white throne, and him that sat on it, from whose face the earth and the heaven fled away; and there was found no place for them. And I saw the dead, small and great, stand before God; and the books were opened: and another book was opened, which is the book of life: and the dead were judged out of those things which were written in the books, according to their works. And the sea gave up the dead which were in it; and death and hell delivered up the dead which were in them: and they were judged every man according to their works. And death and hell were cast into the lake of fire. This is the second death. And whosoever was not found written in the book of life was cast into the lake of fire.

—REVELATION 20:11–15

Where do people go when they die? If they are not washed in the blood of Jesus, they will burn in the lake of fire forever. Someone said, "That sounds absolutely terrible." It is terrible! But there's another side to the story: if they are washed in the blood of Jesus, they go into His everlasting arms forever—in *heaven*!

Some people seem to have a total disregard for the souls of those outside their own circle. They appear unconcerned and even callous about their eternity. When I see people get out of their seats and leave a service *during the altar call*, I want to address them forcefully and personally: "What if the person who is feeling the conviction of the Holy Spirit right now was *your* mother or sister or son?"

Let's make it more personal. What if you had been praying for a loved one for years and just as he was about to lift his hand for prayer, someone pushed by him in an effort to leave the church service early just so that they could get out of the parking lot before everyone else? We have to be sensitive to the Holy Spirit rather than being concerned about our carnal desires—meeting friends for lunch before the buffet closes or rushing home to watch a sports event. The eternal destiny of souls should be our priority.

Many of us have read accounts of those who have witnessed nonbelievers on their deathbeds, going into eternity without Christ. Atheists, agnostics, skeptics and those who have rejected Him experience horror, pain and fear as they depart this life. Many have been heard to scream, "I'm burning! I'm burning! I'm burning in the flames of hell!" Yes, it is a fearsome thing to face eternity without Christ. Death is a separation. Eternal death is an eternal separation from God. Hell is a death that is far more dreadful than the death of the body.

I heard a preacher say that in order to effectively witness for Christ, everyone should go to hell for five minutes. While I understood what he meant, I think that the opposite is also true. I believe every Christian should go to *heaven* for five minutes because once you have tasted of the glories of the heavenly realm, there will be no stopping your witness.

We are getting ready for the harvest. There are people in hell today cursing their preacher because he never told them the truth. And then some people are in hell, regretting the day that they never paid attention to the preacher who *did* tell them the truth! King Agrippa is burning in hell today, and his own words are echoing over and over, *"Almost thou persuadest me to be a Christian"* (Acts 26:28, KJV, emphasis added). The NIV says, *"Do you think that in such a short time you can persuade me to be a Christian?"* (emphasis added).

"I was almost saved, but I was not persuaded." Today, no doubt, King Agrippa regrets that he did not listen to Paul when he still had the opportunity to hear and receive the gospel and be saved from the fires of hell.

CHAPTER THREE

HEAVEN

Heaven is a real place, just as earth is real and hell is real! Heaven is not a place where people float around on fluffy clouds, dressed in white and playing harps or, more absurdly, wearing diapers and holding bows and arrows like little Cupids.

Revelation 21:1-6 gives us a glimpse at the realities of heaven and our life in God's eternal presence if we are washed in the blood of the Lamb.

31

And I saw a new heaven and a new earth: for the first heaven and the first earth were passed away; and there was no more sea. And I John saw the holy city, new Jerusalem, coming down from God out of heaven, prepared as a bride adorned for her husband.

And I heard a great voice out of heaven saying, Behold, the tabernacle of God is with men, and he will dwell with them, and they shall be his people, and God himself shall be with them, and be their God. And God shall wipe away all tears from their eyes; and there shall be no more death, neither sorrow, nor crying, neither shall there be any more pain: for the former things are passed away.

And he that sat upon the throne said, Behold, I make all things new. And he said unto me, Write: for these words are true and faithful. And he said unto me, It is done. I am Alpha and Omega, the beginning and the end. I will give unto him that is athirst of the fountain of the water of life freely.

—KJV

Verse 6 says: *I will give unto him that is athirst of the fountain of the water of life freely* (emphasis added). This is a reality to those who love Jesus even right now— we can drink from this fountain here and now on the earth.

In the last day, that great day of the feast, Jesus stood and cried, saying, If any man thirst, let him come unto me, and drink. He that believeth on me, as the scripture hath said, out of his belly shall flow rivers of living

33

water. (But this spake he of the Spirit, which they that believe on him should receive: for the Holy Ghost was not yet given; because that Jesus was not yet glorified.)

—JOHN 7:37–39, KJV

Thank God for the Holy Spirit! Thank God that we can come and drink of the Living Water that refreshes us, spirit and soul.

Do you have any idea how privileged and honored we are to come and even *begin* to drink of the fountain of life God is already preparing us for us in heaven? There are believers in this world who love Jesus and who love to praise and worship him with their heart and with their voice, and because of this they know what the presence of God feels like. Psalm

22:3 says that the Lord inhabits the praises of His people. He graces us with his presence when we honor Him in praise and worship.

Speaking as a believer, who loves to worship God, I know how wonderful my fellow believers in the body of Christ and I feel when we are in the heights of worship toward our precious Savior. That exultation will be multiplied ten thousand times over when we get to heaven where there will be no restraint of time, or the flesh, or the carnal mind. We will stand there before Him together with the ten thousand times ten thousand from every tribe, language, people, and nation and *worship Him who sits on the throne!*

People who know nothing about the touch of God or the

wonderful presence of God might say, "How boring! You're going to heaven forever. You're going to be worshiping God forever. It's going to be *so boring*." How sad it is that people think that way. They obviously don't know anything about the anointing of the Holy Ghost and have never experienced the power of God! I don't have to go *up* to heaven to know what it is like—I have had a taste of heaven right here on earth—and you can too!

O taste and see that the Lord is good.

—Psalm 34:8, kjv

When you have tasted of the glories of heaven, only one language can adequately express what it is like—the *heavenly language* of the Holy Spirit. Glory to God! (See Isaiah 28:11, Acts 2:2-4, 1 Corinthians 14:2, 1 Corinthians 14:4.)

TO THOSE WHO RECEIVE JESUS CHRIST AS LORD AND SAVIOR AND LIVE OVERCOMING LIVES, THE WORD IS FULL OF WONDERFUL PROMISES.

To those who receive Jesus Christ as Lord and Savior and live overcoming lives, the Word is full of wonderful promises. Revelation 21:7 says, *He that overcometh shall inherit all things; and I will be his God, and he shall be my son* (KJV, emphasis added).

John 1:12 says, *But as many as received him, to them gave he power to become the sons of God* (KJV, emphasis added). We have been given the power by the Word and by the Spirit to become the sons of God! I am so glad I'm saved! I'm so glad I *know*, *without a doubt*, that I'm on my way to heaven.

CHAPTER FOUR

YOUR CHALLENGE

The time to find out where you are going to spend your eternity is not when you have already died and left your body—by then it's too late. God does not want you to spend eternity in torment in hell—that is why He sent Jesus. Because Jesus loves you so much, He came to pay the ultimate price for your sin so that you can have eternal life now and spend your eternity in heaven.

God has a plan for you—a plan for good and for blessing! You can choose your eternal destiny. You can choose life today.

Because you have eternal life the moment you accept Jesus, your life as a child of God is more than just a Sunday morning service. It is twenty-four hours a day, seven days a week, fifty-two weeks of the year! It is not just what you do on Sunday morning that is going to count for eternity. It is what you do Monday, Tuesday, Wednesday, Thursday, Friday, Saturday *and* Sunday.

The things that you do, every hour of the day, every waking moment, not just publicly, but also in secret—your thought life and the attitudes of your heart—all of these things count for eternity. The Bible says that you will give account even of every idle word that you speak (See Matthew 12:36.) You may be careless with your words and your choices, and think that it doesn't matter, but it does matter and it does make a difference.

JESUS CAME TO PAY
THE ULTIMATE PRICE
FOR YOUR SIN.

But the cowardly, the unbelieving, the vile, the murderers, the sexually immoral, those who practice magic arts, the idolaters and all liars—their place will be in the fiery lake of burning sulfur. This is the second death.

—REVELATION 21:8, NIV

The Amplified Version renders Revelation 21:8 this way:

> But as for the cowards and the ignoble and the contemptible and the cravenly lacking in courage and the cowardly submissive, and as for the unbelieving and faithless, and as for the depraved and defiled with abominations, and as for murderers and the lewd and adulterous and the practicers of magic arts and the idolaters (those who give supreme devotion to anyone or anything other than God) and all liars (those who knowingly convey untruth by word or deed)—[all of these shall have] their part in the lake that blazes with fire and brimstone. This is the second death.

Revelation 21:8 talks about eight categories of sinners:

1. The cowardly—those who fear man more than God.

2. The unbelieving and faithless—those who do not believe God's Word or accept His plan of redemption.

3. The depraved and defiled with abominations—those who are dirty and impure in word and deed.

4. Murderers—those who hate others and those who take innocent life.

5. The sexually immoral—the lewd and adulterous, unchaste and unclean men and women.

6. Sorcerers—those who practice magic arts, spiritualists, necromancers, and those who profess to have communications with the dead.

7. Idolaters—those who give supreme devotion to anyone or anything other than God.

8. Liars—those who knowingly convey untruth by word or deed.

Verse eight goes on to explain what happens to these people. "[They] shall have their part in the lake which burns with fire and brimstone, which is the second death."

Now these sins may sound really, really bad to you and you might say, "Well I haven't done such bad things" but in God's eyes, sin is sin. Some people believe that there are big sins and little sins—that certain sins are worse than others, but in God's eyes they are all the same. All sins are on the same level—all sin has the same devastating effect—it cuts us off from God. The Bible says that even those who hate their brothers are murderers, because if you have sinned in your heart or your mind, it is as much sin as if you had actually done it. (See 1 John 3:15.)

You are not a sinner because you have sinned—you sin because you are a sinner. King David said, "I was conceived in sin." (See Psalm 51:5.) Sin has been transferred from generation to generation since the fall of man. Without Jesus, you are a sinner; I am a sinner; every person ever born is a sinner. Therefore every person must also make a decision to accept Jesus in order to be delivered from the power of sin!

After you receive Jesus, the first place you deal with sin is in your thought life, and then it is not so very hard to deal with the sin in your flesh. Of course, there is no way you can deal with sin of any kind on your own. Your own efforts to be righteous and holy before God are as filthy rags. (See Isaiah 64:6.) In other words, they are inadequate and insufficient. That is because you were born a sinner. (See Psalm 51:5.) Romans 3:23 says that, *"all have sinned, and come short of the glory of God"* (KJV, emphasis added). It is impossible for you to come into God's holy presence while you are a sinner. Hebrews 12:14 says that without holiness no man shall see the Lord. You cannot be holy simply by your own efforts. It is impossible for you to come to God on your own terms. You need a Savior—you need someone to stand in the gap for you—to be a bridge between you and God the Father.

Jesus is that bridge—Jesus paid the price, hung on the cross, poured out His blood, bore your sin and diseases in His own body, and died in your place so you could be washed in His blood, saved from your sin, forgiven, acquitted from your guiltiness, and robed in His righteousness. When you believe that Jesus paid the price for you, accept His sacrifice and confess Him as your personal Lord and Savior, you are immediately forgiven and your sins are removed from you as far as the east is from the west. (See Psalm 103:12.) You will not burn in hell, but you will live with the Father in heaven for eternity!

The realization of the seriousness of eternity is what compels us, personally, to be on an airplane every week, carrying the fire of God, doing our best to preach the gospel, demonstrate the power of God, and shake cities, towns, villages, and nations with revival. This is not a game—and we must run now. We must work now, for the night is coming when no man can work. (See John 9:4.) I don't want to get to heaven and hear the Lord say to me, "You could have done a lot more with your time, but you allowed the circumstances of life to hinder you. You allowed your friends, your family members, and circumstances to stop you from fulfilling My plan and My purpose for your life."

The ministry and the call of God is something that is very serious. I want to do whatever it takes. I want to pay the price right now so that when I get on the other side He will look into my eyes and say, "Well done, thou good and faithful servant... enter thou into the joy of thy Lord" (Matt. 25:21). Hallelujah!

CHAPTER FIVE

YOUR CHOICE

The Bible tells us about three kinds of death:

1. Physical death—this is the death we are all familiar with. When your body dies, you just step outside of your body. You still exist, but your body is like a coat that you take off and leave behind.

2. Spiritual death—separation from God—this refers to being spiritually dead, but physically alive. In other words, your body is alive, but

your spirit is separated from God because you have not yet accepted Jesus Christ as your Lord and Savior.

3. Eternal death—this is the third death—when people who are dead spiritually die physically; they will die the third death—*eternal death*. This means they will be separated from God for eternity with no way to make amends or to receive forgiveness.

The good news is that if you receive God's plan of salvation and you are alive spiritually, even if your physical body dies, you will continue to live spiritually, eternally united with God. You must make the choice for eternal life now, while you are alive on the earth. Once you die, there is no going back and no changing your mind. *This is not a myth—this is a fact!*

Believe me, you don't want to push the envelope to test it out. The Bible is very specific about who is going to heaven and who is going to hell, and there is no reason for anyone to be ignorant about this. People who put their trust in Jesus will be saved from hell and welcomed into heaven. People who reject God are in a terrible state. Wickedness takes over their lives. The Bible describes these people this way:

> Because that, when they knew God, they glorified him not as God, neither were thankful; but became vain in their imaginations, and their foolish heart was darkened. Professing

themselves to be wise, they became fools, and changed the glory of the uncorruptible God into an image made like to corruptible man, and to birds, and fourfooted beasts, and creeping things.

Wherefore God also gave them up to uncleanness through the lusts of their own hearts, to dishonour their own bodies between themselves: who changed the truth of God into a lie, and worshipped and served the creature more than the Creator, who is blessed for ever. Amen. For this cause God gave them up unto vile affections: for even their women did change the natural use into that which is against nature:

And likewise also the men, leaving the natural use of the woman, burned in their lust one toward another; men with men working that which is unseemly, and receiving in themselves that recompence of their error which was meet.

—Romans 1:21–27, KJV

This passage above, dear friends, is talking specifically about lesbianism and homosexuality. People say they were born that way, but that is a lie. It is very plain that this is a demon spirit from hell that torments them. They *need* to be delivered and *can* be delivered. The grace and mercy of God is extended to every one of those people if they will receive it.

And even as they did not like to retain God in their knowledge, God gave them over to a reprobate mind, to do those things which are not convenient; being filled with all unrighteousness, fornication, wickedness, covetousness, maliciousness; full of envy, murder, debate, deceit, malignity; whisperers, backbiters, haters of God, despiteful, proud, boasters, inventors of evil things, disobedient to parents,

Without understanding, covenantbreakers, without natural affection, implacable, unmerciful: who knowing the judgment of God, that they which commit such things are worthy of death, not only do the same, but have pleasure in them that do them.

—ROMANS 1:28–32, KJV

The moment the people who do these things die without Christ, they go to hell—God cannot allow them to roam freely.

Even if Jesus walked into hell, they would probably curse Him because of their hatred toward God and the things of God. If Jesus went there to give them another opportunity to trust and receive Him, they would probably reject Him. Why? Because they don't want to serve God— their hearts are possessed by wickedness. We ask, "How could anyone do such things?" Because if we are Christians and we do one little thing wrong, we feel the conviction of the Holy Spirit immediately. We don't take pleasure in sin. That is how we know we are saved and born again. We don't like sin, and we don't want to practice it.

When you are born again, you should not take pleasure in sin in any form—doing it or watching others do it. Even be careful of what kinds of movies and television programs you watch. Protect your thought life and your imagination. Proverbs 23:7 says that what you think is who you are! The things that you think about and meditate on long enough are the things that you will say and do. Sin is a terrible thing, and you must treat it like a horrible disease.

Protect and guard your heart.

Flee also youthful lusts; but pursue righteousness, faith, love, peace with those who call on the Lord out of a pure heart.

—2 Timothy 2:22, nkjv

58

The Bible says that you must *flee* from sin. And you must protect and guard your heart. For some people, that may mean getting rid of certain friends. If you are unable to be a good influence on them and if they are negatively influencing you, then you may have to make a courageous choice and come right out and tell them, "If you won't go to heaven with me, I'm not going to hell with you." You see, there will be a Judgment Day for every single person who lived on earth. Everyone will stand on their own and face God and will have to give an account for their *own* choices—and nobody else's. God is not a respecter of persons, and He will reward each person according to their *own* works.

For the Son of man shall come in the glory of his Father with his angels; and then he shall reward every man according to his works.

—MATTHEW 16:27, KJV

God is a fair and righteous judge. He is kind and merciful and always completely just.

The Bible says:

Your words have been stout against me, saith the LORD. Yet ye say, What have we spoken so much against thee? Ye have said, It is vain to serve God: and what profit is it that we have kept his ordinance, and that we have walked mournfully before the LORD of hosts? And now we call the proud happy; yea, they that work wickedness are set up; yea, they that tempt God are even delivered.

Then they that feared the
LORD spake often one to
another: and the LORD hear-
kened, and heard it, and a book
of remembrance was written
before him for them that feared
the LORD, and that thought
upon his name. And they shall
be mine, saith the LORD of
hosts, in that day when I make
up my jewels; and I will spare
them, as a man spareth his own
son that serveth him. Then
shall ye return, and discern
between the righteous and the
wicked, between him that
serveth God and him that
serveth him not.

—MALACHI 3:13–18, KJV

For, behold, the day cometh,
that shall burn as an oven; and
all the proud, yea, and all that do
wickedly, shall be stubble: and

61

the day that cometh shall burn them up, saith the LORD of hosts, that it shall leave them neither root nor branch. But unto you that fear my name shall the Sun of righteousness arise with healing in his wings; and ye shall go forth, and grow up as calves of the stall. And ye shall tread down the wicked; for they shall be ashes under the soles of your feet in the day that I shall do this, saith the LORD of hosts.

—MALACHI 4:1–3

Sometimes people get mad at God because they think that life is unfair and that God has not treated them right. They are convinced that when things go wrong—it is all God's fault! It is funny how these same people, who blame God for the bad things in their lives, don't go out of their way to praise and thank God when things go really well in their lives. Realize that what you sow you *will* reap. (See Galatians 6:7.) Keep your heart right, do the right thing, and in the end God will bless you and reward you for your faithfulness. He will also reward those who fight against Him—they will be cut off without a remedy.

Judgment Day is a disaster for the wicked, but those who trust in Jesus are ushered into heaven, which is so beautiful and majestic that words can barely begin to describe it. God allowed the apostle John to see a revelation of heaven, and this is what he wrote:

And there came unto me one of the seven angels which had the seven vials full of the seven last plagues, and talked with me, saying, Come hither, I will show thee the bride, the Lamb's wife. And he carried me away in the spirit to a great and high mountain, and showed me that great city, the holy Jerusalem, descending out of heaven from God, having the glory of God: and her light was like unto a stone most precious, even like a jasper stone, clear as crystal;

And had a wall great and high, and had twelve gates, and at the gates twelve angels, and names written thereon, which are the names of the twelve tribes of the children of Israel: On the east three gates; on the north three gates; on the south three gates; and on the west three gates. And the wall of the

city had twelve foundations,
and in them the names of the
twelve apostles of the Lamb.

And he that talked with me
had a golden reed to measure
the city, and the gates thereof,
and the wall thereof. And the
city lieth foursquare, and the
length is as large as the breadth:
and he measured the city with
the reed, twelve thousand fur-
longs. The length and the
breadth and the height of it are
equal. And he measured the
wall thereof, an hundred and
forty and four cubits, according
to the measure of a man, that is,
of the angel.

And the building of the wall
of it was of jasper: and the city
was pure gold, like unto clear
glass. And the foundations of the
wall of the city were garnished
with all manner of precious
stones. The first foundation was

jasper; the second, sapphire; the third, a chalcedony; the fourth, an emerald; the fifth, sardonyx; the sixth, sardius; the seventh, chrysolite; the eighth, beryl; the ninth, a topaz; the tenth, a chrysoprasus; the eleventh, a jacinth; the twelfth, an amethyst.

And the twelve gates were twelve pearls; every several gate was of one pearl: and the street of the city was pure gold, as it were transparent glass. And I saw no temple therein: for the Lord God Almighty and the Lamb are the temple of it. And the city had no need of the sun, neither of the moon, to shine in it; for the glory of God did lighten it, and the Lamb is the light thereof.

And the nations of them which are saved shall walk in the light of it: and the kings of the earth do bring their glory and honour into it. And the gates of it shall not be shut at all by day: for there shall be no night there. And they shall bring the glory and honour of the nations into it. And there shall in no wise enter into it any thing that defileth, neither whatsoever worketh abomination, or maketh a lie: but they which are written in the Lamb's book of life.

—REVELATION 21:9–27, KJV

IS YOUR NAME WRITTEN IN THE LAMB'S BOOK OF LIFE?

Notice that the only ones who will be allowed to enter into the holy city are they whose names are written in the Lamb's Book of

Life. I want to ask you a question: "Is your name written in the Lamb's Book of Life?"

You may ask, "Brother Rodney, what do I have to do to have my name written down in the Lamb's Book of Life? Where do I go from here? How do I make heaven and not hell my eternal home?" The Word of God is very clear on this. The Bible says:

> And as Moses lifted up the serpent in the wilderness, even so must the Son of man be lifted up: That whosoever believeth in him should not perish, but have eternal life. For God so loved the world, that he gave his only begotten Son, that whosoever believeth in him should not perish, but have everlasting life.

68

For God sent not his Son into the world to condemn the world; but that the world through him might be saved. He that believeth on him is not condemned: but he that believeth not is condemned already, because he hath not believed in the name of the only begotten Son of God.

—JOHN 3:14–18, KJV

That if thou shalt confess with thy mouth the Lord Jesus, and shalt believe in thine heart that God hath raised him from the dead, thou shalt be saved. For with the heart man believeth unto righteousness; and with the mouth confession is made unto salvation.

—ROMANS 10:9–10, KJV,
EMPHASIS ADDED

Verily, verily, I say unto you, He that heareth my word, and

believeth on him that sent me,
hath everlasting life, and shall
not come into condemnation;
but is passed from death unto
life.

—John 5:24, kjv

To have your name in the
Lamb's Book of Life, first of all,
you need to receive Jesus as your
Lord and Savior. Secondly, you
need to cut yourself off from
those things that could pull you
back into the sinful lifestyle of
which you have already been forgiven. Jesus took the punishment
for your sin, but that doesn't mean
you can keep on sinning. Once
you are born again, sin has no
more power over you, and by the
power of the Holy Spirit, you can
walk free from sin. The Bible

70

speaks very plainly about things you and I can do to make sure that heaven is our eternal home. We don't have to live in guilt, condemnation, and judgment, but we do have to deal with sin.

If you are a Christian and you sin, you will still be a Christian—you will still have a relationship with God—He will still be your Father. However, your fellowship with Him will be affected. On the other hand, if you willingly continue to give in to sin, it may bring you to a place where your heart becomes hardened toward God, you cut yourself off from Him, and then your relationship with Him is adversely affected. So it is very important to guard your heart and deal with sin immediately. Don't give it any place in your life.

And if thy hand offend thee, cut it off: it is better for thee to enter into life maimed, than having two hands to go into hell, into the fire that never shall be quenched: where their worm dieth not, and the fire is not quenched. And if thy foot offend thee, cut it off: it is better for thee to enter halt into life, than having two feet to be cast into hell, into the fire that never shall be quenched: where their worm dieth not, and the fire is not quenched.

And if thine eye offend thee, pluck it out: it is better for thee to enter into the kingdom of God with one eye, than having two eyes to be cast into hell fire: where their worm dieth not, and the fire is not quenched. For every one shall be salted with fire, and every sacrifice shall be salted with salt. Salt is good: but

if the salt have lost his saltness,
wherewith will ye season it?
Have salt in yourselves, and
have peace one with another.

—MARK 9:43–50, KJV

And if thy right eye offend thee,
pluck it out, and cast it from
thee…And if thy right hand
offend thee, cut it off, and cast
it from thee: for it is profitable
for thee that one of thy members should perish, and not that
thy whole body should be cast
into hell.

—MATTHEW 5:29–30, KJV

Wherefore if thy hand or thy
foot offend thee, cut them off,
and cast them from thee: it is
better for thee to enter into life
halt or maimed, rather than
having two hands or two feet to
be cast into everlasting fire. And
if thine eye offend thee, pluck it

out, and cast it from thee: it is better for thee to enter into life with one eye, rather than having two eyes to be cast into hell fire.

—Matthew 18:8–9, kjv

Now God is not asking people to pluck their eyes out of their head, but He would rather you go to heaven than go to hell for eternity. It would be better to be blind and go to heaven than be sighted and go to hell. But you don't have to cut off parts of your body; rather, you need to get rid of anything that is causing you to sin— and you should do it immediately.

I heard the story of a doctor who had such a problem with lust that in desperation he castrated himself. However, lust is a spiritual problem. And spiritual problems cannot be solved by human effort, no matter how radical the effort may be. The Holy Spirit has come to empower Christians to overcome their problems. The Holy Spirit will change your heart so completely that your eyes won't want to look at unrighteous things, and your thought processes will be totally transformed. You will no longer want to be involved in sin. God gives us grace to take care of spiritual things on a spiritual level rather than mutilating ourselves physically. His plan is better.

The Bible speaks very plainly about things you and I can do to make sure that heaven is our eternal home. We don't have to live in guilt, condemnation, and judgment, but we *do* have to deal with sin. We need to put our flesh under and renew our minds with the Word of God. The Bible says, "And be renewed in the spirit of your mind…put on the new man, which after God is created in righteousness and true holiness" (Eph. 4:23–24, KJV). The Bible also says that the church is cleansed with the "washing of the water by the word" (Eph. 5:26, KJV).

> (For the weapons of our warfare are not carnal, but mighty through God to the pulling down of strong holds;) Casting down imaginations, and every high thing that exalteth itself against the knowledge of God, and bringing into captivity every thought to the obedience of Christ.
>
> —2 CORINTHIANS 10:4–5, KJV

We need to take every thought captive. Don't even entertain evil thoughts for a moment. Be ready to attack those thoughts and take them captive, in the name of Jesus Christ.

Something as seemingly innocuous as television or the Internet can be a tool for drawing us into sin. There is so much garbage on television and on the Internet now that we have to actively filter everything we look at and listen to. We can't just sit passively and take in whatever comes across the air. If you have had difficulty with pornography, lust, and perversion, you need to do whatever it takes to deal with the problem. Don't let it suck you right down to hell. Don't play around with that kind of thing. It is like the bank of a slippery creek—if you fool around with it, you will eventually slip and slide all the way down into the mud. You are dealing with eternal issues! The choices you make concerning these things have eternal consequences. If you need to get help, swallow your pride and get help! Let the power of the Holy Spirit set you free from that bondage. I urge you to do whatever it takes to get free.

CHAPTER SIX

WHERE ARE
YOU GOING?

I ask you, my friend, if you died right now, where would you spend eternity? You don't have to go to a devil's hell. That is the good news of the gospel of the Lord Jesus Christ. Today you can make a decision and take the road that leads to eternal life. Today you can surrender your life to Jesus and say, "Lord, here I come! I give my life to you. I give my all to you." He will not reject you or push you away. He stands with arms wide open. He says, "Come."

Are you a Christian who has been touched by the Spirit of the Lord in the last several years? Do you remember the feeling that you had when the anointing of God touched you? Wasn't it wonderful! Well, heaven is greater than that. That was just a taste of how it will be all of the time.

YOU HAVE THE CHOICE

OF WHERE YOU WILL

SPEND ETERNITY.

Have you ever been in a place of remorse, feeling so distraught that you were hitting your head against the wall? Think back and try to remember how dreadful it felt. Then think about this: hell is far worse than that.

80

Heaven and hell are distinct opposites. And while you are still living, you have the choice of where you will spend eternity. You are in charge of your destiny! *The choice is yours.*

Today, as in Noah's day, the ark is here, but a mighty storm is coming and it will cause a great flood. I see the clouds on the horizon; I hear the distant thunder; I see the flashes of lightning. The gangplank is down. You can come! You can come running into the ark, and you can be saved today. The day will come when the door of the ark will be closed, and by then it will be too late. Today is the day of salvation! Today is the day of deliverance! Today, if you will hear His voice, harden not your heart!

Several years ago, there was a film made entitled *What Dreams May Come.* In the film, heaven and hell were all according to your own imagination. Whatever you thought and believed—that is what you experienced. The truth is that it is no dream, but it is very real. The real question is, *what realities will come?* There is a heaven, and there is a hell. Where will you go when you die? Where will you spend eternity?

I hope you have been asking yourself these questions as you have been reading this book. If you are not born again, if you don't know Jesus as your personal Lord and Savior, and if the spirit of God has been talking to you and moving on your heart, now is the time to say, "Lord, here I am.

Forgive me of all my sins. I surrender my all to you."

WHERE WILL YOU SPEND ETERNITY?

If you were once on fire for God but you have become lukewarm, you need to rekindle your relationship with Him. Those little embers aren't enough—God wants to light that fire again on the inside of you!

Maybe, dear reader, you are one of those who is not sure where you stand with God, and He is talking to you about making sure of your salvation.

There is no reason why you cannot be absolutely sure of your salvation today. Make the choice to call on Him, and you will be amazed at how quickly He answers your prayer. Jesus loves you, and He is just waiting to hear you say, "Jesus, here I am. Help me." This is your day of opportunity, and I thank God that He will meet you as you run to Him!

THIS IS YOUR REALITY!

You can pray and receive Jesus Christ right now:

Heavenly Father,

I come to You now in the precious name of Your Son, Jesus. Lord, You said in Your Word that if I confess with my mouth, "Jesus is Lord," and believe in my heart that God has raised Him from the dead, I will be saved. So, Father, right now, I confess that Jesus is my Lord and my Savior. Jesus, I ask You to come into my heart right now. Take out the stony heart and put in a heart of flesh. I turn my back on the world and follow You, Lord Jesus. Wash me, cleanse me, change me, fill me, use me. Let me never be the same again. Thank You, Lord, for shedding Your blood for me. Thank You, Lord for dying for me. Thank You that on the third day You rose again for me. Thank You that you are coming back again for me. I confess that Jesus Christ has come in the flesh. He is my Lord and my Savior. I will never be the same again. In Jesus' name, amen.

POSTSCRIPT

If you have been blessed and challenged by this book, please write to us here at our Tampa office or email us at testimonies@revival.com

We would love to hear from you. If you were stirred up and challenged to change and allow God to do His work in you, we pray that God would use you in a wonderful way to touch a lost and dying world.

Write to:
Revival Ministries International
P.O. Box 292888
Tampa, FL 33687

You can also reach me at:
www.revival.com/prayer/testimony.aspx

or

call 1(813) 971-9999

For souls and another Great Spiritual Awakening in America,
Dr. Rodney Howard-Browne

The River at Tampa Bay Church
Easter Sunday, April 2014

The River at Tampa Bay Church
The Main Event, May 2014

The River at Tampa Bay Church
The Main Event, May 2014

The River at Tampa Bay Church
The Main Event, September 2013

The River at Tampa Bay Church
The First River Fest, January 2013

The River at Tampa Bay Church
River Fest, February 2013

The River at Tampa Bay Church
River Fest, August 2013

The River at Tampa Bay Church
Thanksgiving Fest, November 2013

Revival Ministries International
Campmeeting Lakeland Summer 2013

Revival Ministries International
Campmeeting Lakeland Summer 2013

The Great Awakening Live Broadcast
Night 200, July 2011

The Great Awakening Live Broadcast
Night 108, April 2011

Good News Umlazi
Umlazi, South Africa, 2005

Good News Soweto

Soweto, South Africa, 2004

The Early Years
Rodney and Adonica Howard-Browne

Rodney Howard-Browne
Singapore, 1995

The Howard-Browne Family
(Rodney, Adonica, Kirsten, Kelly & Kenneth)

About

Drs. Rodney and Adonica Howard-Browne

Drs. Rodney and Adonica Howard-Browne are the founders of The River at Tampa Bay Church, River Bible Institute, River School of Worship, and River School of Government in Tampa, Florida.

Rodney and Adonica have been called by God to reach out to the nations – whilst keeping America as their primary mission field. Their heart is to see the Church – the Body of Christ – revived, and the lost won to Christ. They have conducted a number of mass crusades and many outreaches, but their heart is also to train and equip others to bring in the harvest – from one-on-one evangelism to outreaches that reach tens, hundreds, thousands and even tens of thousands. Every soul matters and every salvation is a victory for the kingdom of God!

In December of 1987, Rodney, along with his wife, Adonica, and their three children, Kirsten, Kelly and Kenneth, moved from their native land, South Africa, to the United States – called by God as missionaries from Africa to America. The Lord had spoken through Rodney in a word of prophecy and declared: "As America has sown missionaries over the last 200 years, I am going to raise up people from other nations to come to the United States of America. I am sending a mighty revival to America."

In April of 1989, the Lord sent a revival of signs and wonders and miracles that began in a church in Clifton Park, New York, that has continued until today, resulting in thousands of people being touched and changed as they encounter the presence of the living God! God is still moving today – saving, healing, delivering, restoring, and setting free!

Drs. Rodney and Adonica's second daughter, Kelly, was born with an incurable lung disease called Cystic Fibrosis. This demonic disease slowly destroyed her lungs. Early on Christmas morning 2002, at the age of eighteen, she ran out of lung capacity and breathed out her last breath. They placed her into the arms of her Lord and Savior and then vowed a vow. First, they vowed that the devil would pay for what he had done to their family. Secondly, they vowed to do everything in their power, with the help of the Lord, to win 100 million souls to Jesus and to put $1 billion into world missions and the harvest of souls.

With a passion for souls and a passion to revive and mobilize the body of Christ, Drs. Rodney and Adonica have conducted soul-winning efforts throughout America and other countries with "Good News" campaigns, R.M.I. Revivals, and the Great Awakening Tours (G.A.T.). As a result, millions have come to Christ and tens of thousands of believers have been revived and mobilized to preach the Gospel of Jesus Christ. So far, around the world, over 9,523,000 people have made decisions for Jesus Christ through this ministry.

Drs. Rodney and Adonica thank God for America and are grateful to have become Naturalized Citizens of the United States of America. When they became U.S. citizens, in 2008 and 2004 respectively, they took the United States Oath of Allegiance, which declares, "... I will support and defend the Constitution and laws of the United States of America against all enemies, foreign and domestic..." They took this oath to heart and intend to keep it. They love America, are praying for this country, and are trusting God to see another Great Awakening sweep across this land. Truly, the only hope for America is another Great Spiritual Awakening. For more information about the ministry of Drs. Rodney and Adonica Howard-Browne, please, visit www.revival.com

Other Books and Resources:

Books

The Touch of God

The Reality of Life After Death

Seeing Jesus as He Really Is

The Curse Is Not Greater than the
Blessing

The Coat My Father Gave Me

How to Increase and Release the
Anointing

School of the Spirit

The Anointing

Fresh Oil from Heaven

Manifesting the Holy Ghost

Audio CDs

The Touch of God: The Anointing

Good News New York

Knowing the Person of the Holy Spirit

Prayer Time

Stewardship

The Love Walk by Dr. Adonica
Howard-Browne

Weapons of Our Warfare

Becoming One Flesh by Drs. Rodney
& Adonica
Howard-Browne

Faith

Flowing in the Holy Ghost

How to Hear the Voice of God
How to Flow in the Anointing
Igniting the Fire
In Search of the Anointing
Prayer that Moves Mountains
Running the Heavenly Race
The Holy Spirit, His Purpose & Power
The Power to Create Wealth
Walking in Heaven's Light
All These Blessings
A Surplus of Prosperity
The Joy of the Lord Is My Strength
Prayer Secrets
Communion – The Table of the Lord
My Roadmap
My Mission – My Purpose
My Heart
My Family
My Worship
Decreeing Faith
Ingredients of Revival
Fear Not
Matters of the Heart by Dr. Adonica
Howard-Browne
My Treasure
My Absolutes
My Father
My Crowns

My Comforter & Helper
Renewing the Mind
Seated in High Places
Triumphant Entry
Merchandising and Trafficking the
Anointing
My Prayer Life
My Jesus
Seeing Jesus as He Really Is
Exposing the World's System
Living in the Land of Visions &
Dreams

DVDs
God's Glory Manifested through
Special Anointings
Good News New York
Jerusalem Ablaze
The Mercy of God by Dr. Adonica
Howard-Browne
Are You a Performer of a Minister?
Revival at ORU Volume 1
Revival at ORU Volume 2
Revival at ORU Volume 3
The Realms of God
Singapore Ablaze
The Coat My Father Gave Me
Have You Ever Wondered What Jesus
Was Like?

There Is a Storm Coming (Recorded live from Good News New York)

Budapest, Hungary Ablaze

The Camels Are Coming

Power Evangelism by Dr. Rodney Howard-Browne & The Great Awakening Team

Taking Cities in the Land of Giants

Renewing the Mind

Triumphant Entry

Merchandising and Trafficking the Anointing

Doing Business with God

Music

Nothing Is Impossible

Nothing Is Impossible Soundtrack

By His Stripes

Run with Fire

The Sweet Presence of Jesus

Eternity with Kelly Howard-Browne

Live from the River

You're Such a Good God to Me

Revival Down Under

Howard-Browne Family Christmas

Haitian Praise

He Lives

No Limits

Anointed – The Decade of the '80s

Information Page

Please, visit revival.com for our latest updates and news. Many of our services are live online. Additionally, many of our recorded services are available on Video on Demand.

For a listing of Drs. Rodney and Adonica Howard-Browne's products and itinerary, please, visit revival.com

To download the soul-winning tools for free, please, visit revival.com and click on Soul-winning Tools or go to www.revival.com/soulwinning-tools.24.1.html

 www.facebook.com/pages/Rodney-Adonica-Howard-Browne/31553452437

 www.twitter.com/rhowardbrowne

 www.youtube.com/rodneyhowardbrowne

The River at Tampa Bay Church

Pastors Rodney and Adonica Howard-Browne (Senior Pastors & Founders)

Address: 3738 River International Dr. Tampa, FL 33610

The River at Tampa Bay Church was founded on December 1, 1996. At the close of 1996, the Lord planted within Pastors Rodney and Adonica's heart the vision and desire to start a church in Tampa. With a heart for the lost and to minister to those who had been touched by revival, they implemented that vision and began The River at Tampa Bay, with the motto, "Church with a Difference."

Over 500 people joined them for the first Sunday morning service on December 1, 1996. Over the years, the membership has grown and the facilities have changed, yet these three things have remained constant since the church's inception...dynamic praise and worship, anointed preaching and teaching of the Word, and powerful demonstrations of the Holy Spirit and power. The Lord spoke to Pastor Rodney's heart to feed the people, touch the people, and love the people. With this in mind and heart, the goal of the River is:

- To become a model revival church where people from all over the world can come and be touched by God. Once they have been not only touched, but changed, they are ready to be launched out into the harvest field with the anointing of God.

- To have a church that is multi-racial, representing a cross section of society from rich to poor from all nations, bringing people to a place of maturity in their Christian walk.

- To see the lost, the backslidden and the unsure come to a full assurance of their salvation.

- To be a home base for Revival Ministries International and all of its arms. A base offering strength and support to the vision of RMI to see America shaken with the fires of revival, then to take that fire to the far-flung corners of the globe.

- To break the mold of religious tradition and thinking.

- To be totally dependent upon the Holy Spirit for His leading and guidance as we lead others deeper into the River of God.

- Our motto: Church with a Difference.

For The River at Tampa Bay's service times and directions, please, visit revival.com or call 1 (813) 971-9999.

The River Bible Institute

The River Bible Institute (RBI) is a place where men and women of all ages, backgrounds and experiences can gather together to study and experience the glory of God. The River Bible Institute is not a traditional Bible school. It is a Holy Ghost training center, birthed specifically for those whose strongest desire is to know Christ and to make Him known.

The vision for The River Bible Institute is plain: To train men and women in the spirit of revival for ministry in the 21st century. The school was birthed in 1997 with a desire to train up revivalists for the 21st Century. It is a place where the Word of God and the Holy Spirit come together to produce life, birth ministries, and launch them out. The River Bible Institute is a place where ministries are sent to the far-flung corners of the globe to spread revival and to bring in a harvest of souls for the kingdom of God.

While preaching in many nations and regions of the world, Dr. Rodney Howard-Browne has observed that all the people of the earth have one thing in common: A desperate need for the genuine touch of God. From the interior of Alaska through the bush country of Africa, to the outback villages of Australia to the cities of North America, people are tired of religion and ritualistic worship. They are crying out for the reality of His presence. The River Bible Institute is dedicated to training believers how to live, minister, and flow in the anointing.

The Word will challenge those attending the Institute to find clarity in their calling, and be changed by the awesome presence of God. This is the hour of God's power. Not just for the full-time minister, but for all of God's people who are hungry for more. Whether you are a housewife or an aspiring evangelist, The River Bible Institute will deepen your relationship and experience in the Lord, and provide you with a new perspective on how to reach others with God's life-changing power.

You can be saturated in the Word and the Spirit of God at The River Bible Institute. It is the place where you will be empowered to reach your high calling and set your world on fire with revival.

For more information about the River Bible Institute, please, visit revival.com or call 1 (813) 899-0085 or 1 (813) 971-9999.

The River School of Worship

The River School of Worship (RSW) is where ability becomes accountability, talent becomes anointing and ambition becomes vision.

It has been Drs. Rodney and Adonica Howard-Browne's dream for many years to provide a place where men and women of all ages, backgrounds and experiences could gather together to study and experience the glory of God. The River School of Worship is not a traditional music school. It is a training center birthed specifically for those whose strongest desire is to worship in Spirit and in Truth, and where the Word of God and the Holy Spirit come together to produce life, birth ministries, and launch them out.

The Word will challenge those of you attending to find clarity in your calling, and be changed by the awesome presence of God. The River School of Worship will deepen your relationship and experience in the Lord, and provide you with new perspective on how to reach others with God's life-changing power. You can be saturated in the Word and the Spirit of God at the River School of Worship. It is the place where you will be empowered to reach your high calling and set your world on fire with revival.

For more information about the River School of Worship, please, visit

revival.com or call 1 (813) 899-0085 or 1 (813) 971-9999.

The River School of Government

Moreover, you shall choose able men from all the people — God-fearing men of truth who hate unjust gain — and place them over thousands, hundreds, fifties, and tens, to be their rulers. Exodus 18:21 AMP

The River School of Government (RSG) has been founded as a result of the corruption we see in the current government system and the need to raise up godly individuals with personal and public integrity to boldly take up positions of leadership in our nation. For hundreds of years the Constitution of the United States of America, the supreme law of the land, has stood as a bulwark of righteousness, to protect the rights of its citizens. However, there have been attacks, from many quarters, all designed to neutralize the Constitution and to progressively remove citizen's rights.

There is a great need to raise up individuals who will run for office in the United States of America, from the very bottom all the way to the highest level of government, who will honor and stand up for both the integrity of the Constitution and the integrity of God's Word. If we are going to see America changed for the good, we have to get back to her founding principles, which were laid out by the founding fathers at her inception. This is the heart and soul and primary focus of the River School of Government.

The River School of Government will work to expose the enemies of our sovereignty and Constitution. The student will be trained in every area of governmental leadership and responsibility, and upon successful graduation will be entrusted with specific positions, tasks and responsibilities, each according to their ability and calling. The River School of Government's goal is not to raise up career politicians, who will abuse their position for personal gain or for personal power, but to raise up people who will govern according to solid godly principles and who will continue to faithfully defend the individual rights and freedoms that are guaranteed by both the Constitution and God's Word.

The River School of Government is non-partisan and has one objective – to raise up people in government, who are armed with a solid foundation in the Constitution, God's Holy Word, and the power of the Holy Spirit - to take America back! We believe that the Lord will help us to accomplish this goal of taking America back, with a well-defined four, eight, twelve, sixteen, and twenty-year plan, springing out of a third Great Spiritual Awakening!

For more information about the River School of Government, please, call 1(813) 899-0085 or 1(813) 971-9999 or email us at rsg@revival.com

God Wants to Use You to Bring in the Harvest of Souls!

The Great Commission, "Go ye into all the world and preach the gospel to every creature," is for every believer to take personally. Every believer is to be an announcer of the Good News Gospel. When the Gospel is preached, people have an encounter with Jesus. Jesus is the only One Who can change the heart of a man, woman, child, and nation! Here is a tool to assist you in sharing the Gospel with others. It is called the Gospel Soul Winning Script. Please, just read it! Read the front and the back of it to others and you will see many come to Christ because the Gospel is the power of God (see Romans 1:16).

Please, visit revival.com, click on Soul-winning Tools, and review the many tools and videos that are freely available to help you bring in the harvest of souls. It's harvest time!

THE GOSPEL, SOUL-WINNING —SCRIPT—

Has anyone ever told you that God loves you and that He has a wonderful plan for your life? I have a real quick, but important question to ask you. If you were to die this very second, do you know for sure, beyond a shadow of a doubt, that you would go to Heaven? [If "Yes"— Great, why would you say "Yes"? (If they respond with anything but "I have Jesus in my heart" or something similar to that, PROCEED WITH SCRIPT) or "No" or "I hope so" PROCEED WITH SCRIPT.]

Let me quickly share with you what the Holy Bible reads. It reads "for all have sinned and come short of the glory of God" and "for the wages of sin is death, but the gift of God is eternal life through Jesus Christ our Lord". The Bible also reads, "For whosoever shall call upon the name of the Lord shall be saved". And you're a "whosoever" right? Of course you are; all of us are.

continued on reverse side—

119

I'm going to say a quick prayer for you. Lord, bless (FILL IN NAME) and his/her family with long and healthy lives. Jesus, make Yourself real to him/her and do a quick work in his/her heart. If (FILL IN NAME) has not received Jesus Christ as his/her Lord and Savior, I pray he/she will do so now.

(FILL IN NAME), if you would like to receive the gift that God has for you today, say this after me with your heart and lips out loud. Dear Lord Jesus, come into my heart. Forgive me of my sin. Wash me and cleanse me. Set me free. Jesus, thank You that You died for me. I believe that You are risen from the dead and that You're coming back again for me. Fill me with the Holy Spirit. Give me a passion for the lost, a hunger for the things of God and a holy boldness to preach the gospel of Jesus Christ. I'm saved; I'm born again, I'm forgiven and I'm on my way to Heaven because I have Jesus in my heart.

As a minister of the gospel of Jesus Christ, I tell you today that all of your sins are forgiven. Always remember to run to God and not from God because He loves you and has a great plan for your life.

[Invite them to your church and get follow up info: name, address, & phone number.]

Revival Ministries International
P.O. Box 292888 · Tampa, FL 33687
(813) 971-9999 · www.revival.com